# T HE

## H OUSEHOLD

#### P URCHASED

# CONGRATULATIONS!

You've decided to start a home renovation project. Now what?

Use this organizer to track your remodeling projects and ideas room by room and keep information in one place.

Each section includes lists for the room measurements and requirements, space to jot down decor and style ideas, and a sketchpad area for furniture or renovation designs. There is also a Master Checklist section at the end to list all of the steps, permits, materials, etc you will need to complete the project.

Good luck and happy renovation!

# QUICK TIPS
## for Home Renovation Projects

1. Create a budget before designing

2. Decide when the project is too complex, and you need to hire a contractor

3. "Interview" contractors first. Choose based on their experience and if you can communicate with them

4. Buy materials before work begins

5. If the contractor says your ideas won't work, have them explain why and describe alternatives

6. There will be surprises. Add extra time and money to your project plan

# 1 Room Name

_____

**Renovating is not about making a
house look new...
it's about making it home.**

# Room Vision

## Room Requirements

- [ ] L x W x H _____
- [ ] _____
- [ ] _____
- [ ] _____
- [ ] _____
- [ ] _____
- [ ] _____
- [ ] _____
- [ ] _____
- [ ] _____
- [ ] _____

## Decor & Style Ideas

_____

_____

_____

_____

_____

_____

_____

_____

_____

_____

_____

_____

## Sketchpad

# Progress Tracker

## Weekly Goals

☐ _____

☐ _____

☐ _____

☐ _____

☐ _____

☐ _____

☐ _____

☐ _____

☐ _____

☐ _____

## Questions & Issues

_____

_____

_____

_____

_____

_____

_____

_____

_____

_____

## To-Do

•

•

•

•

•

•

•

•

•

•

## Material Shopping List

☐ _____

☐ _____

☐ _____

☐ _____

☐ _____

☐ _____

☐ _____

☐ _____

☐ _____

☐ _____

# Progress Tracker

## Weekly Goals

- ☐ _____
- ☐ _____
- ☐ _____
- ☐ _____
- ☐ _____
- ☐ _____
- ☐ _____
- ☐ _____
- ☐ _____
- ☐ _____

## Questions & Issues

_____

_____

_____

_____

_____

_____

_____

_____

_____

_____

## To-Do

- •
- •
- •
- •
- •
- •
- •
- •
- •

## Material Shopping List

- ☐ _____
- ☐ _____
- ☐ _____
- ☐ _____
- ☐ _____
- ☐ _____
- ☐ _____
- ☐ _____
- ☐ _____
- ☐ _____

# Progress Tracker

## Weekly Goals

- ☐ _____
- ☐ _____
- ☐ _____
- ☐ _____
- ☐ _____
- ☐ _____
- ☐ _____
- ☐ _____
- ☐ _____
- ☐ _____

## Questions & Issues

_____
_____
_____
_____
_____
_____
_____
_____
_____
_____

## To-Do

- •
- •
- •
- •
- •
- •
- •
- •
- •

## Material Shopping List

- ☐ _____
- ☐ _____
- ☐ _____
- ☐ _____
- ☐ _____
- ☐ _____
- ☐ _____
- ☐ _____
- ☐ _____
- ☐ _____

# Progress Tracker

## Weekly Goals

- [ ] _____
- [ ] _____
- [ ] _____
- [ ] _____
- [ ] _____
- [ ] _____
- [ ] _____
- [ ] _____
- [ ] _____
- [ ] _____

## Questions & Issues

_____

_____

_____

_____

_____

_____

_____

_____

_____

_____

## To-Do

- 
- 
- 
- 
- 
- 
- 
- 
- 

## Material Shopping List

- [ ] _____
- [ ] _____
- [ ] _____
- [ ] _____
- [ ] _____
- [ ] _____
- [ ] _____
- [ ] _____
- [ ] _____
- [ ] _____

# Notes

Sketchpad

# Notes

Sketchpad

# 2 Room Name
_____

**Ideally, live in a house for one year
before you remodel.**

# Room Vision

## Room Requirements

- [ ] L x W x H _____
- [ ] _____
- [ ] _____
- [ ] _____
- [ ] _____
- [ ] _____
- [ ] _____
- [ ] _____
- [ ] _____
- [ ] _____
- [ ] _____

## Decor & Style Ideas

_____

_____

_____

_____

_____

_____

_____

_____

_____

_____

_____

## Sketchpad

# Progress Tracker

## Weekly Goals

- [ ] _____
- [ ] _____
- [ ] _____
- [ ] _____
- [ ] _____
- [ ] _____
- [ ] _____
- [ ] _____
- [ ] _____
- [ ] _____

## Questions & Issues

_____
_____
_____
_____
_____
_____
_____
_____
_____
_____

## To-Do

-
-
-
-
-
-
-
-
-
-

## Material Shopping List

- [ ] _____
- [ ] _____
- [ ] _____
- [ ] _____
- [ ] _____
- [ ] _____
- [ ] _____
- [ ] _____
- [ ] _____
- [ ] _____

# Progress Tracker

## Weekly Goals

- [ ] _____
- [ ] _____
- [ ] _____
- [ ] _____
- [ ] _____
- [ ] _____
- [ ] _____
- [ ] _____
- [ ] _____
- [ ] _____

## Questions & Issues

_____

_____

_____

_____

_____

_____

_____

_____

_____

_____

## To-Do

- 
- 
- 
- 
- 
- 
- 
- 
- 

## Material Shopping List

- [ ] _____
- [ ] _____
- [ ] _____
- [ ] _____
- [ ] _____
- [ ] _____
- [ ] _____
- [ ] _____
- [ ] _____
- [ ] _____

# Progress Tracker

## Weekly Goals

- [ ] _____
- [ ] _____
- [ ] _____
- [ ] _____
- [ ] _____
- [ ] _____
- [ ] _____
- [ ] _____
- [ ] _____
- [ ] _____

## Questions & Issues

_____
_____
_____
_____
_____
_____
_____
_____
_____
_____

## To-Do

- 
- 
- 
- 
- 
- 
- 
- 
- 

## Material Shopping List

- [ ] _____
- [ ] _____
- [ ] _____
- [ ] _____
- [ ] _____
- [ ] _____
- [ ] _____
- [ ] _____
- [ ] _____
- [ ] _____

# Progress Tracker

## Weekly Goals

- [ ] _____
- [ ] _____
- [ ] _____
- [ ] _____
- [ ] _____
- [ ] _____
- [ ] _____
- [ ] _____
- [ ] _____
- [ ] _____

## Questions & Issues

_____

_____

_____

_____

_____

_____

_____

_____

_____

_____

## To-Do

- 
- 
- 
- 
- 
- 
- 
- 
- 

## Material Shopping List

- [ ] _____
- [ ] _____
- [ ] _____
- [ ] _____
- [ ] _____
- [ ] _____
- [ ] _____
- [ ] _____
- [ ] _____
- [ ] _____

# Notes

Sketchpad

# Notes

Sketchpad

# 3 Room Name

_____

**Renovation will be messy,
but it will be worth it.**

# Room Vision

## Room Requirements

- [ ] L x W x H _____
- [ ] _____
- [ ] _____
- [ ] _____
- [ ] _____
- [ ] _____
- [ ] _____
- [ ] _____
- [ ] _____
- [ ] _____
- [ ] _____

## Decor & Style Ideas

_____
_____
_____
_____
_____
_____
_____
_____
_____
_____
_____
_____

## Sketchpad

# Progress Tracker

## Weekly Goals

- [ ] _____
- [ ] _____
- [ ] _____
- [ ] _____
- [ ] _____
- [ ] _____
- [ ] _____
- [ ] _____
- [ ] _____
- [ ] _____

## Questions & Issues

_____

_____

_____

_____

_____

_____

_____

_____

_____

_____

## To-Do

- 
- 
- 
- 
- 
- 
- 
- 
- 

## Material Shopping List

- [ ] _____
- [ ] _____
- [ ] _____
- [ ] _____
- [ ] _____
- [ ] _____
- [ ] _____
- [ ] _____
- [ ] _____
- [ ] _____

# Progress Tracker

## Weekly Goals

- [ ] _____
- [ ] _____
- [ ] _____
- [ ] _____
- [ ] _____
- [ ] _____
- [ ] _____
- [ ] _____
- [ ] _____
- [ ] _____

## Questions & Issues

_____
_____
_____
_____
_____
_____
_____
_____
_____

## To-Do

- 
- 
- 
- 
- 
- 
- 
- 
- 

## Material Shopping List

- [ ] _____
- [ ] _____
- [ ] _____
- [ ] _____
- [ ] _____
- [ ] _____
- [ ] _____
- [ ] _____
- [ ] _____
- [ ] _____

# Progress Tracker

## Weekly Goals

- [ ] _____
- [ ] _____
- [ ] _____
- [ ] _____
- [ ] _____
- [ ] _____
- [ ] _____
- [ ] _____
- [ ] _____
- [ ] _____

## Questions & Issues

_____

_____

_____

_____

_____

_____

_____

_____

_____

_____

## To-Do

- 
- 
- 
- 
- 
- 
- 
- 
- 

## Material Shopping List

- [ ] _____
- [ ] _____
- [ ] _____
- [ ] _____
- [ ] _____
- [ ] _____
- [ ] _____
- [ ] _____
- [ ] _____
- [ ] _____

# Progress Tracker

## Weekly Goals

- [ ] _____
- [ ] _____
- [ ] _____
- [ ] _____
- [ ] _____
- [ ] _____
- [ ] _____
- [ ] _____
- [ ] _____
- [ ] _____

## Questions & Issues

_____
_____
_____
_____
_____
_____
_____
_____
_____
_____

## To-Do

- 
- 
- 
- 
- 
- 
- 
- 
- 
- 

## Material Shopping List

- [ ] _____
- [ ] _____
- [ ] _____
- [ ] _____
- [ ] _____
- [ ] _____
- [ ] _____
- [ ] _____
- [ ] _____
- [ ] _____

# Notes

Sketchpad

# Notes

## Sketchpad

# 4 Room Name

_____

**Renovators don't need a sense of humor,
but it helps.**

# Room Vision

## Room Requirements

- [ ] L x W x H _____
- [ ] _____
- [ ] _____
- [ ] _____
- [ ] _____
- [ ] _____
- [ ] _____
- [ ] _____
- [ ] _____
- [ ] _____
- [ ] _____

## Decor & Style Ideas

_____

_____

_____

_____

_____

_____

_____

_____

_____

_____

## Sketchpad

# Progress Tracker

## Weekly Goals

- ☐ _____
- ☐ _____
- ☐ _____
- ☐ _____
- ☐ _____
- ☐ _____
- ☐ _____
- ☐ _____
- ☐ _____
- ☐ _____

## Questions & Issues

_____

_____

_____

_____

_____

_____

_____

_____

_____

_____

## To-Do

- •
- •
- •
- •
- •
- •
- •
- •
- •

## Material Shopping List

- ☐ _____
- ☐ _____
- ☐ _____
- ☐ _____
- ☐ _____
- ☐ _____
- ☐ _____
- ☐ _____
- ☐ _____
- ☐ _____

# Progress Tracker

## Weekly Goals

- [ ] _____
- [ ] _____
- [ ] _____
- [ ] _____
- [ ] _____
- [ ] _____
- [ ] _____
- [ ] _____
- [ ] _____
- [ ] _____

## Questions & Issues

_____
_____
_____
_____
_____
_____
_____
_____
_____
_____

## To-Do

- 
- 
- 
- 
- 
- 
- 
- 
- 

## Material Shopping List

- [ ] _____
- [ ] _____
- [ ] _____
- [ ] _____
- [ ] _____
- [ ] _____
- [ ] _____
- [ ] _____
- [ ] _____
- [ ] _____

# Progress Tracker

## Weekly Goals

- [ ] _____
- [ ] _____
- [ ] _____
- [ ] _____
- [ ] _____
- [ ] _____
- [ ] _____
- [ ] _____
- [ ] _____
- [ ] _____

## Questions & Issues

_____
_____
_____
_____
_____
_____
_____
_____
_____
_____

## To-Do

- 
- 
- 
- 
- 
- 
- 
- 
- 

## Material Shopping List

- [ ] _____
- [ ] _____
- [ ] _____
- [ ] _____
- [ ] _____
- [ ] _____
- [ ] _____
- [ ] _____
- [ ] _____
- [ ] _____

# Progress Tracker

## Weekly Goals

- [ ] _____
- [ ] _____
- [ ] _____
- [ ] _____
- [ ] _____
- [ ] _____
- [ ] _____
- [ ] _____
- [ ] _____
- [ ] _____

## Questions & Issues

_____

_____

_____

_____

_____

_____

_____

_____

_____

_____

## To-Do

- 
- 
- 
- 
- 
- 
- 
- 
- 

## Material Shopping List

- [ ] _____
- [ ] _____
- [ ] _____
- [ ] _____
- [ ] _____
- [ ] _____
- [ ] _____
- [ ] _____
- [ ] _____
- [ ] _____

# Notes

Sketchpad

# Notes

Sketchpad

# 5 Room Name

_____

**Choose the things you really love,
remodel with those in mind.**

# Room Vision

## Room Requirements

- [ ] L x W x H _____
- [ ] _____
- [ ] _____
- [ ] _____
- [ ] _____
- [ ] _____
- [ ] _____
- [ ] _____
- [ ] _____
- [ ] _____
- [ ] _____

## Decor & Style Ideas

_____

_____

_____

_____

_____

_____

_____

_____

_____

_____

_____

## Sketchpad

# Progress Tracker

## Weekly Goals

- [ ] _____
- [ ] _____
- [ ] _____
- [ ] _____
- [ ] _____
- [ ] _____
- [ ] _____
- [ ] _____
- [ ] _____
- [ ] _____

## Questions & Issues

_____

_____

_____

_____

_____

_____

_____

_____

_____

_____

## To-Do

- 
- 
- 
- 
- 
- 
- 
- 
- 

## Material Shopping List

- [ ] _____
- [ ] _____
- [ ] _____
- [ ] _____
- [ ] _____
- [ ] _____
- [ ] _____
- [ ] _____
- [ ] _____
- [ ] _____

# Progress Tracker

## Weekly Goals

- [ ] _____
- [ ] _____
- [ ] _____
- [ ] _____
- [ ] _____
- [ ] _____
- [ ] _____
- [ ] _____
- [ ] _____
- [ ] _____

## Questions & Issues

_____

_____

_____

_____

_____

_____

_____

_____

_____

_____

## To-Do

-
-
-
-
-
-
-
-
-
-

## Material Shopping List

- [ ] _____
- [ ] _____
- [ ] _____
- [ ] _____
- [ ] _____
- [ ] _____
- [ ] _____
- [ ] _____
- [ ] _____
- [ ] _____

# Progress Tracker

## Weekly Goals

- [ ] _____
- [ ] _____
- [ ] _____
- [ ] _____
- [ ] _____
- [ ] _____
- [ ] _____
- [ ] _____
- [ ] _____
- [ ] _____

## Questions & Issues

_____

_____

_____

_____

_____

_____

_____

_____

_____

_____

## To-Do

- 
- 
- 
- 
- 
- 
- 
- 
- 

## Material Shopping List

- [ ] _____
- [ ] _____
- [ ] _____
- [ ] _____
- [ ] _____
- [ ] _____
- [ ] _____
- [ ] _____
- [ ] _____
- [ ] _____

# Progress Tracker

## Weekly Goals

- [ ] _____
- [ ] _____
- [ ] _____
- [ ] _____
- [ ] _____
- [ ] _____
- [ ] _____
- [ ] _____
- [ ] _____
- [ ] _____

## Questions & Issues

_____

_____

_____

_____

_____

_____

_____

_____

_____

_____

## To-Do

- 
- 
- 
- 
- 
- 
- 
- 
- 

## Material Shopping List

- [ ] _____
- [ ] _____
- [ ] _____
- [ ] _____
- [ ] _____
- [ ] _____
- [ ] _____
- [ ] _____
- [ ] _____
- [ ] _____

# Notes

Sketchpad

# Notes

---

## Sketchpad

# 6 Room Name

_____

**Stay positive during setbacks,
the project won't last forever!**

# Room Vision

## Room Requirements

- [ ] L x W x H _____
- [ ] _____
- [ ] _____
- [ ] _____
- [ ] _____
- [ ] _____
- [ ] _____
- [ ] _____
- [ ] _____
- [ ] _____
- [ ] _____

## Decor & Style Ideas

_____

_____

_____

_____

_____

_____

_____

_____

_____

_____

_____

## Sketchpad

# Progress Tracker

## Weekly Goals

- [ ] _____
- [ ] _____
- [ ] _____
- [ ] _____
- [ ] _____
- [ ] _____
- [ ] _____
- [ ] _____
- [ ] _____
- [ ] _____

## Questions & Issues

_____

_____

_____

_____

_____

_____

_____

_____

_____

_____

## To-Do

- 
- 
- 
- 
- 
- 
- 
- 
- 

## Material Shopping List

- [ ] _____
- [ ] _____
- [ ] _____
- [ ] _____
- [ ] _____
- [ ] _____
- [ ] _____
- [ ] _____
- [ ] _____

# Progress Tracker

## Weekly Goals

- ☐ _____
- ☐ _____
- ☐ _____
- ☐ _____
- ☐ _____
- ☐ _____
- ☐ _____
- ☐ _____
- ☐ _____
- ☐ _____

## Questions & Issues

_____

_____

_____

_____

_____

_____

_____

_____

_____

_____

## To-Do

- •
- •
- •
- •
- •
- •
- •
- •
- •
- •

## Material Shopping List

- ☐ _____
- ☐ _____
- ☐ _____
- ☐ _____
- ☐ _____
- ☐ _____
- ☐ _____
- ☐ _____
- ☐ _____
- ☐ _____

# Progress Tracker

## Weekly Goals

- ☐ _____
- ☐ _____
- ☐ _____
- ☐ _____
- ☐ _____
- ☐ _____
- ☐ _____
- ☐ _____
- ☐ _____
- ☐ _____

## Questions & Issues

_____

_____

_____

_____

_____

_____

_____

_____

_____

_____

## To-Do

- •
- •
- •
- •
- •
- •
- •
- •
- •
- •

## Material Shopping List

- ☐ _____
- ☐ _____
- ☐ _____
- ☐ _____
- ☐ _____
- ☐ _____
- ☐ _____
- ☐ _____
- ☐ _____
- ☐ _____

# Progress Tracker

## Weekly Goals

- ☐ _____
- ☐ _____
- ☐ _____
- ☐ _____
- ☐ _____
- ☐ _____
- ☐ _____
- ☐ _____
- ☐ _____
- ☐ _____

## Questions & Issues

_____

_____

_____

_____

_____

_____

_____

_____

_____

_____

## To-Do

- •
- •
- •
- •
- •
- •
- •
- •
- •
- •

## Material Shopping List

- ☐ _____
- ☐ _____
- ☐ _____
- ☐ _____
- ☐ _____
- ☐ _____
- ☐ _____
- ☐ _____
- ☐ _____
- ☐ _____

# Notes

Sketchpad

# Notes

## Sketchpad

# 7 Room Name

_____

Listen to other renovation stories,
hearing them can help you plan.

# Room Vision

## Room Requirements

- [ ] L x W x H _____
- [ ] _____
- [ ] _____
- [ ] _____
- [ ] _____
- [ ] _____
- [ ] _____
- [ ] _____
- [ ] _____
- [ ] _____
- [ ] _____

## Decor & Style Ideas

_____
_____
_____
_____
_____
_____
_____
_____
_____
_____
_____

## Sketchpad

# Progress Tracker

## Weekly Goals

- ☐ _____
- ☐ _____
- ☐ _____
- ☐ _____
- ☐ _____
- ☐ _____
- ☐ _____
- ☐ _____
- ☐ _____
- ☐ _____

## Questions & Issues

_____

_____

_____

_____

_____

_____

_____

_____

_____

_____

## To-Do

- •
- •
- •
- •
- •
- •
- •
- •
- •

## Material Shopping List

- ☐ _____
- ☐ _____
- ☐ _____
- ☐ _____
- ☐ _____
- ☐ _____
- ☐ _____
- ☐ _____
- ☐ _____
- ☐ _____

# Progress Tracker

## Weekly Goals

- [ ] _____
- [ ] _____
- [ ] _____
- [ ] _____
- [ ] _____
- [ ] _____
- [ ] _____
- [ ] _____
- [ ] _____
- [ ] _____

## Questions & Issues

_____

_____

_____

_____

_____

_____

_____

_____

_____

_____

## To-Do

- 
- 
- 
- 
- 
- 
- 
- 

## Material Shopping List

- [ ] _____
- [ ] _____
- [ ] _____
- [ ] _____
- [ ] _____
- [ ] _____
- [ ] _____
- [ ] _____
- [ ] _____
- [ ] _____

# Progress Tracker

## Weekly Goals

- ☐ _____
- ☐ _____
- ☐ _____
- ☐ _____
- ☐ _____
- ☐ _____
- ☐ _____
- ☐ _____
- ☐ _____
- ☐ _____

## Questions & Issues

_____
_____
_____
_____
_____
_____
_____
_____
_____
_____

## To-Do

- •
- •
- •
- •
- •
- •
- •
- •
- •

## Material Shopping List

- ☐ _____
- ☐ _____
- ☐ _____
- ☐ _____
- ☐ _____
- ☐ _____
- ☐ _____
- ☐ _____
- ☐ _____
- ☐ _____

# Progress Tracker

## Weekly Goals

☐ _____

☐ _____

☐ _____

☐ _____

☐ _____

☐ _____

☐ _____

☐ _____

☐ _____

☐ _____

## Questions & Issues

_____

_____

_____

_____

_____

_____

_____

_____

_____

_____

## To-Do

- 
- 
- 
- 
- 
- 
- 
- 
- 

## Material Shopping List

☐ _____

☐ _____

☐ _____

☐ _____

☐ _____

☐ _____

☐ _____

☐ _____

☐ _____

☐ _____

# Notes

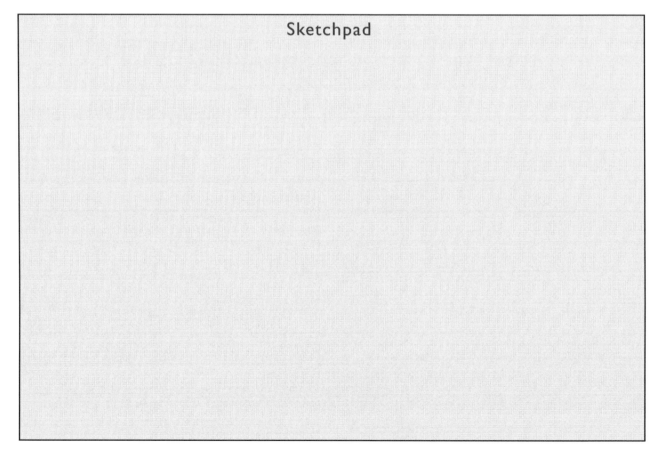

Sketchpad

# Notes

---

## Sketchpad

# 8 Room Name

_____

**Don't be afraid to ask your
contractor for references.**

# Room Vision

## Room Requirements

- [ ] L x W x H _____
- [ ] _____
- [ ] _____
- [ ] _____
- [ ] _____
- [ ] _____
- [ ] _____
- [ ] _____
- [ ] _____
- [ ] _____
- [ ] _____

## Decor & Style Ideas

_____

_____

_____

_____

_____

_____

_____

_____

_____

_____

_____

_____

## Sketchpad

# Progress Tracker

## Weekly Goals

- [ ] _____
- [ ] _____
- [ ] _____
- [ ] _____
- [ ] _____
- [ ] _____
- [ ] _____
- [ ] _____
- [ ] _____
- [ ] _____

## Questions & Issues

_____
_____
_____
_____
_____
_____
_____
_____
_____
_____
_____

## To-Do

- 
- 
- 
- 
- 
- 
- 
- 
- 

## Material Shopping List

- [ ] _____
- [ ] _____
- [ ] _____
- [ ] _____
- [ ] _____
- [ ] _____
- [ ] _____
- [ ] _____
- [ ] _____
- [ ] _____

# Progress Tracker

## Weekly Goals

- ☐ _____
- ☐ _____
- ☐ _____
- ☐ _____
- ☐ _____
- ☐ _____
- ☐ _____
- ☐ _____
- ☐ _____
- ☐ _____

## Questions & Issues

_____
_____
_____
_____
_____
_____
_____
_____
_____
_____
_____
_____

## To-Do

- •
- •
- •
- •
- •
- •
- •
- •
- •

## Material Shopping List

- ☐ _____
- ☐ _____
- ☐ _____
- ☐ _____
- ☐ _____
- ☐ _____
- ☐ _____
- ☐ _____
- ☐ _____
- ☐ _____

# Progress Tracker

## Weekly Goals

☐ _____

☐ _____

☐ _____

☐ _____

☐ _____

☐ _____

☐ _____

☐ _____

☐ _____

☐ _____

## Questions & Issues

_____

_____

_____

_____

_____

_____

_____

_____

_____

_____

## To-Do

- 
- 
- 
- 
- 
- 
- 
- 

## Material Shopping List

☐ _____

☐ _____

☐ _____

☐ _____

☐ _____

☐ _____

☐ _____

☐ _____

☐ _____

☐ _____

# Progress Tracker

## Weekly Goals

☐ _____

☐ _____

☐ _____

☐ _____

☐ _____

☐ _____

☐ _____

☐ _____

☐ _____

☐ _____

## Questions & Issues

_____

_____

_____

_____

_____

_____

_____

_____

_____

_____

_____

## To-Do

- 
- 
- 
- 
- 
- 
- 
- 
- 

## Material Shopping List

☐ _____

☐ _____

☐ _____

☐ _____

☐ _____

☐ _____

☐ _____

☐ _____

☐ _____

☐ _____

# Notes

_____
_____
_____
_____
_____
_____
_____
_____
_____
_____
_____
_____
_____

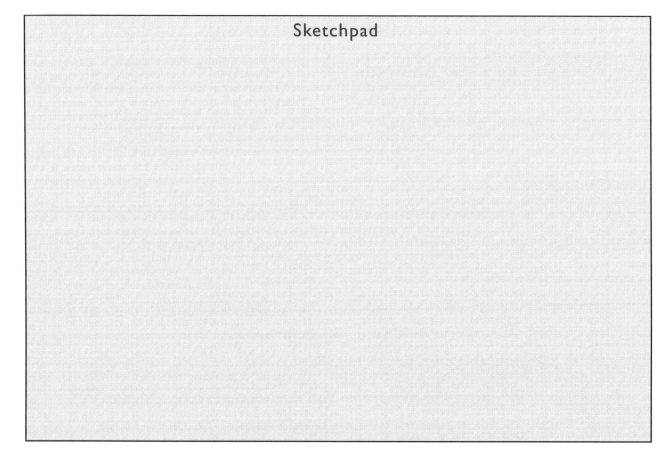

Sketchpad

# Notes

_____

_____

_____

_____

_____

_____

_____

_____

_____

_____

_____

_____

## Sketchpad

# 9 Room Name

_____

**Schedule contractors in off-peak seasons,
you can usually get lower rates.**

# Room Vision

## Room Requirements

- [ ] L x W x H _____
- [ ] _____
- [ ] _____
- [ ] _____
- [ ] _____
- [ ] _____
- [ ] _____
- [ ] _____
- [ ] _____
- [ ] _____
- [ ] _____

## Decor & Style Ideas

_____

_____

_____

_____

_____

_____

_____

_____

_____

_____

_____

## Sketchpad

# Progress Tracker

## Weekly Goals

- ☐ _____
- ☐ _____
- ☐ _____
- ☐ _____
- ☐ _____
- ☐ _____
- ☐ _____
- ☐ _____
- ☐ _____
- ☐ _____

## Questions & Issues

_____

_____

_____

_____

_____

_____

_____

_____

_____

_____

## To-Do

- •
- •
- •
- •
- •
- •
- •
- •

## Material Shopping List

- ☐ _____
- ☐ _____
- ☐ _____
- ☐ _____
- ☐ _____
- ☐ _____
- ☐ _____
- ☐ _____
- ☐ _____
- ☐ _____

# Progress Tracker

## Weekly Goals

- ☐ _____
- ☐ _____
- ☐ _____
- ☐ _____
- ☐ _____
- ☐ _____
- ☐ _____
- ☐ _____
- ☐ _____
- ☐ _____

## Questions & Issues

_____
_____
_____
_____
_____
_____
_____
_____
_____
_____

## To-Do

- •
- •
- •
- •
- •
- •
- •
- •
- •

## Material Shopping List

- ☐ _____
- ☐ _____
- ☐ _____
- ☐ _____
- ☐ _____
- ☐ _____
- ☐ _____
- ☐ _____
- ☐ _____
- ☐ _____

# Progress Tracker

## Weekly Goals

- ☐ _____
- ☐ _____
- ☐ _____
- ☐ _____
- ☐ _____
- ☐ _____
- ☐ _____
- ☐ _____
- ☐ _____
- ☐ _____

## Questions & Issues

_____

_____

_____

_____

_____

_____

_____

_____

_____

## To-Do

- •
- •
- •
- •
- •
- •
- •
- •
- •

## Material Shopping List

- ☐ _____
- ☐ _____
- ☐ _____
- ☐ _____
- ☐ _____
- ☐ _____
- ☐ _____
- ☐ _____
- ☐ _____
- ☐ _____

# Progress Tracker

## Weekly Goals

- ☐ _____
- ☐ _____
- ☐ _____
- ☐ _____
- ☐ _____
- ☐ _____
- ☐ _____
- ☐ _____
- ☐ _____
- ☐ _____

## Questions & Issues

_____

_____

_____

_____

_____

_____

_____

_____

_____

_____

## To-Do

- •
- •
- •
- •
- •
- •
- •
- •
- •

## Material Shopping List

- ☐ _____
- ☐ _____
- ☐ _____
- ☐ _____
- ☐ _____
- ☐ _____
- ☐ _____
- ☐ _____
- ☐ _____
- ☐ _____

# Notes

_____

_____

_____

_____

_____

_____

_____

_____

_____

_____

_____

_____

Sketchpad

# 10 Room Name

_____

**Create a reno-free zone,
a tidy relaxation space helps.**

# Room Vision

## Room Requirements

- [ ] L x W x H _____
- [ ] _____
- [ ] _____
- [ ] _____
- [ ] _____
- [ ] _____
- [ ] _____
- [ ] _____
- [ ] _____
- [ ] _____
- [ ] _____

## Decor & Style Ideas

_____

_____

_____

_____

_____

_____

_____

_____

_____

_____

## Sketchpad

# Progress Tracker

## Weekly Goals

- ☐ _____
- ☐ _____
- ☐ _____
- ☐ _____
- ☐ _____
- ☐ _____
- ☐ _____
- ☐ _____
- ☐ _____
- ☐ _____

## Questions & Issues

_____

_____

_____

_____

_____

_____

_____

_____

_____

_____

_____

## To-Do

- •
- •
- •
- •
- •
- •
- •
- •
- •
- •

## Material Shopping List

- ☐ _____
- ☐ _____
- ☐ _____
- ☐ _____
- ☐ _____
- ☐ _____
- ☐ _____
- ☐ _____
- ☐ _____
- ☐ _____

# Progress Tracker

## Weekly Goals

- ☐ _____
- ☐ _____
- ☐ _____
- ☐ _____
- ☐ _____
- ☐ _____
- ☐ _____
- ☐ _____
- ☐ _____
- ☐ _____

## Questions & Issues

_____

_____

_____

_____

_____

_____

_____

_____

_____

_____

## To-Do

- •
- •
- •
- •
- •
- •
- •
- •
- •
- •

## Material Shopping List

- ☐ _____
- ☐ _____
- ☐ _____
- ☐ _____
- ☐ _____
- ☐ _____
- ☐ _____
- ☐ _____
- ☐ _____
- ☐ _____

# Progress Tracker

## Weekly Goals

- ☐ _____
- ☐ _____
- ☐ _____
- ☐ _____
- ☐ _____
- ☐ _____
- ☐ _____
- ☐ _____
- ☐ _____
- ☐ _____

## Questions & Issues

_____

_____

_____

_____

_____

_____

_____

_____

_____

_____

## To-Do

- •
- •
- •
- •
- •
- •
- •
- •
- •

## Material Shopping List

- ☐ _____
- ☐ _____
- ☐ _____
- ☐ _____
- ☐ _____
- ☐ _____
- ☐ _____
- ☐ _____
- ☐ _____
- ☐ _____

# Progress Tracker

## Weekly Goals

- [ ] _____
- [ ] _____
- [ ] _____
- [ ] _____
- [ ] _____
- [ ] _____
- [ ] _____
- [ ] _____
- [ ] _____
- [ ] _____

## Questions & Issues

_____

_____

_____

_____

_____

_____

_____

_____

_____

_____

## To-Do

- 
- 
- 
- 
- 
- 
- 
- 
- 

## Material Shopping List

- [ ] _____
- [ ] _____
- [ ] _____
- [ ] _____
- [ ] _____
- [ ] _____
- [ ] _____
- [ ] _____
- [ ] _____
- [ ] _____

# Notes

Sketchpad

# Notes

Sketchpad

# Notes

_____

_____

_____

_____

_____

_____

_____

_____

_____

_____

_____

_____

Sketchpad

# Notes

## Sketchpad

# Notes

Sketchpad

# Notes

Sketchpad

# Notes

# Notes

## Sketchpad

# Notes

# Notes

Sketchpad

# Notes

Sketchpad

# Notes

Sketchpad

# Master Checklist

Have   Need

☐ ☐ _____

☐ ☐ _____

☐ ☐ _____

☐ ☐ _____

☐ ☐ _____

☐ ☐ _____

☐ ☐ _____

☐ ☐ _____

☐ ☐ _____

☐ ☐ _____

☐ ☐ _____

☐ ☐ _____

☐ ☐ _____

☐ ☐ _____

☐ ☐ _____

☐ ☐ _____

☐ ☐ _____

☐ ☐ _____

☐ ☐ _____

☐ ☐ _____

☐ ☐ _____

☐ ☐ _____

# Master Checklist

Have   Need

☐   ☐ _____

☐   ☐ _____

☐   ☐ _____

☐   ☐ _____

☐   ☐ _____

☐   ☐ _____

☐   ☐ _____

☐   ☐ _____

☐   ☐ _____

☐   ☐ _____

☐   ☐ _____

☐   ☐ _____

☐   ☐ _____

☐   ☐ _____

☐   ☐ _____

☐   ☐ _____

☐   ☐ _____

☐   ☐ _____

☐   ☐ _____

☐   ☐ _____

☐   ☐ _____

# Master Checklist

Have  Need

☐ ☐ _____

☐ ☐ _____

☐ ☐ _____

☐ ☐ _____

☐ ☐ _____

☐ ☐ _____

☐ ☐ _____

☐ ☐ _____

☐ ☐ _____

☐ ☐ _____

☐ ☐ _____

☐ ☐ _____

☐ ☐ _____

☐ ☐ _____

☐ ☐ _____

☐ ☐ _____

☐ ☐ _____

☐ ☐ _____

☐ ☐ _____

☐ ☐ _____

☐ ☐ _____

☐ ☐ _____

# Master Checklist

Have   Need

☐ ☐ _____

☐ ☐ _____

☐ ☐ _____

☐ ☐ _____

☐ ☐ _____

☐ ☐ _____

☐ ☐ _____

☐ ☐ _____

☐ ☐ _____

☐ ☐ _____

☐ ☐ _____

☐ ☐ _____

☐ ☐ _____

☐ ☐ _____

☐ ☐ _____

☐ ☐ _____

☐ ☐ _____

☐ ☐ _____

☐ ☐ _____

☐ ☐ _____

☐ ☐ _____

☐ ☐ _____

# Master Checklist

Have   Need

☐   ☐   _____

☐   ☐   _____

☐   ☐   _____

☐   ☐   _____

☐   ☐   _____

☐   ☐   _____

☐   ☐   _____

☐   ☐   _____

☐   ☐   _____

☐   ☐   _____

☐   ☐   _____

☐   ☐   _____

☐   ☐   _____

☐   ☐   _____

☐   ☐   _____

☐   ☐   _____

☐   ☐   _____

☐   ☐   _____

☐   ☐   _____

☐   ☐   _____

☐   ☐   _____

# Master Checklist

Have   Need

☐   ☐ _____

☐   ☐ _____

☐   ☐ _____

☐   ☐ _____

☐   ☐ _____

☐   ☐ _____

☐   ☐ _____

☐   ☐ _____

☐   ☐ _____

☐   ☐ _____

☐   ☐ _____

☐   ☐ _____

☐   ☐ _____

☐   ☐ _____

☐   ☐ _____

☐   ☐ _____

☐   ☐ _____

☐   ☐ _____

☐   ☐ _____

☐   ☐ _____

☐   ☐ _____

☐   ☐ _____

# Master Checklist

| Have | Need | |
|------|------|---|
| ☐ | ☐ | _____ |
| ☐ | ☐ | _____ |
| ☐ | ☐ | _____ |
| ☐ | ☐ | _____ |
| ☐ | ☐ | _____ |
| ☐ | ☐ | _____ |
| ☐ | ☐ | _____ |
| ☐ | ☐ | _____ |
| ☐ | ☐ | _____ |
| ☐ | ☐ | _____ |
| ☐ | ☐ | _____ |
| ☐ | ☐ | _____ |
| ☐ | ☐ | _____ |
| ☐ | ☐ | _____ |
| ☐ | ☐ | _____ |
| ☐ | ☐ | _____ |
| ☐ | ☐ | _____ |
| ☐ | ☐ | _____ |
| ☐ | ☐ | _____ |
| ☐ | ☐ | _____ |
| ☐ | ☐ | _____ |
| ☐ | ☐ | _____ |

# Master Checklist

Have    Need

☐    ☐    _____

☐    ☐    _____

☐    ☐    _____

☐    ☐    _____

☐    ☐    _____

☐    ☐    _____

☐    ☐    _____

☐    ☐    _____

☐    ☐    _____

☐    ☐    _____

☐    ☐    _____

☐    ☐    _____

☐    ☐    _____

☐    ☐    _____

☐    ☐    _____

☐    ☐    _____

☐    ☐    _____

☐    ☐    _____

☐    ☐    _____

☐    ☐    _____

☐    ☐    _____

Printed in Great Britain
by Amazon